HECHIZERA
Sus Sultry Spells

by

Diosa Xochiquetzalcóatl

EDITORIAL
RAÍCES

Rancho Cucamonga
CA. U.S. 91730

Copyright © 2022 Adriana Citlali Brenes-Rios.

All rights reserved. No part of this publication may be reproduced, distributed, or transmitted in any form or by any means, including photocopying, recording, or other electronic or mechanical methods, without the prior written permission of the author, except in the case of brief quotations embodied in critical reviews and certain other noncommercial uses permitted by copyright law.

To request permissions, you may contact the author at temachtianicitlali@gmail.com.

Any references to historical events, real people, or real places are used fictitiously. Names, characters, places, and situations are products of the author's imagination. In other words—*le puedo echar más salsa a mis tacos porque al fin y al cabo son mis tacos.*

Interior book design by Adriana Citlali Brenes-Rios.
Cover design by Adriana Citlali Brenes-Rios.
Edited by Masiel M. Corona Santos.

ISBN: 979-8-218-04824-2

Library of Congress Control Number: 2022915153

TABLE OF CONTENTS

PROLOGUE

*Say You Do

- Do You Believe in Magic? 15

SUGAR AND SPICE

*...And Sometimes Nice

- The Color of the Adriatic Sea 21
- Eudaemonic 23
- The Unfleshing of Mere Mortals 24

*Catch Her if You Can

- When the West Met His Wild 29
- Love in the Times of Quarantine 31
- Odd Night 33

*Sweet to the Sweet

- I'm in Love with 37
- Hipoglucemia 38
- Chocorrol y Bon-Bon 40

*I Scream for Ice Cream

- I'd Rather Have Ice Cream for Dinner 43
- Fría 44
- Just Two Tubs of Ice Cream 45

*Café con Pan

- Café de la olla 49

- Lil Red and Mr. Lobo 50

- San Pan 51

*Pan con Café

- Moist 55

- El Jaguar 56

- Café de la olla (sequela) 57

*Esta Noche, Cena Pancha

- Engage 61

- Palabras sabias 62

- Ambrosia 63

*Y Pancho También

- La lengua del amor 67

- Pandemic Pussy 69

- Ya cállate y cómeme 70

*Viva México

- La Rumorosa 73

- Momma Likes Mexican 74

- Ché chilangos chachareros 75

*La Gira

- Blood Transfusion 79

- ¡Arriba Jalisco! 80

- Trippin' 81

***Enchanted**

- Incantation 85

- Eros and Psyche 86

- Impregnate Me 87

***Brisas No, Solo Torbellinos**

- Lo que queda grabado 91

- El cuento de una estrella fugaz 92

- The Big Bang 94

***So Above, Below**

- In Excelsis Deo 97

- Want to Be 98

- Del Mar 99

***P is for Puta**

- Pencaminosa 103

- Poly 104

- P de perdición 105

***Al Rojo Vivo**

- Scarlet Skies 109

- Sangria Seductions 112

- Raw 113

*The Freaks Come Out at Night

- The Bewitching Hour 117

- La Mari Mota 118

- Nightmare 120

TRUCHA

*Proceed with Precaución

- Warning 127

- Cuidado 128

- Beware! 129

*S-P-E-L-L-I-N-G Be

- A Plague on Both Your Houses 133

- Orthography 134

- Became 135

*Did Someone Say Bruja?

- Leta-mía 139

- Today, I Killed a Tarantula 141

- El embrujado 142

*Welcome to My Jungle

- La selva te llama 145

- Felina 146

- Bottom of My Soles 147

*You Thought
- Shady Magik 151
- En camino 152
- Voodoo 154

*Unstoppable
- Candle Work 157
- Black Spiders 158
- Armada 159

*Holy, Holy, Holy
- El padre y la puta 163
- El cuento más pequeño 164
- All Hail St. Michaela 165

*Truth Hurts
- Ya no sé ni cómo ponerle 169
- La dieta 3T 170
- Sentí-miento 171

*Justicia
- St. Michaela Presiding in the Case of Libra vs. *el Mudo* 175
- Todo con medida 176
- The X m-en-tourage 177

*La Tequilera
- La Cruda Realidad 181

- ¡Salucita! 182

- AMF 183

*Hasta la Pasta

- Diez amantes 187

- Las hieles de enero 190

- ¡Tan! ¡Tan! 191

*A la Chingada

- Butcher 195

- Evanesco! 196

- Soiled 198

*La Santa Muerte

- La Valentina 201

- Conejo Blas 202

- Era del signo Libra 203

*These Ghosts Ain't Friendly

- The Scariest of All 207

- The Haunting 208

- Ghosted 210

*Don't Close Your Eyes

- I've Finally Awakened from that Illusion 215

- Camarón que se duerme 216

- Testament 217

*Thy Queendom Come

    - Not the Same 221

    - Soul-Awe 222

    - El reinado de la Diosa no tiene fin 223

*El Pilón (porque el reinado no tiene fin - obvio)

    - Entre las grietas 227

EPILOGUE

*I Told You So

    -Missing the Magic? 233

P.S.A.

*The Effects of Excessive Chile

    -Reflujo 239

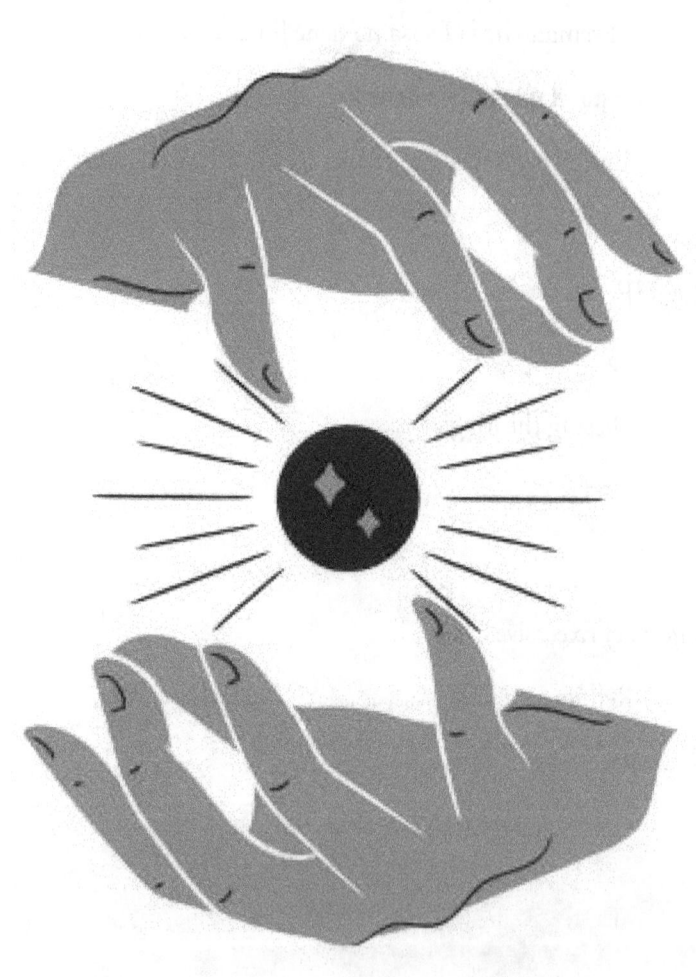

Say You Do

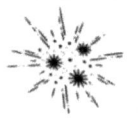

Do You Believe in Magic?

Do you believe in magic? Please tell me that you do.
Do you believe in crystal balls and colors of mystical hues?

Do you believe I could creep your dreams to lay in bed beside you;
that I can stalk the way you walk and your every waking move?

Do you believe I could cause you pain if you proved to be untrue;
begin to make you feel insane and hopelessly lose your cool?

Do you believe that I could wrap you up and make you be my boo;
that I can keep you in my bed until the very next full moon?

'Tis true! 'Tis true! But I don't play the fool.
I don't work for the dark forces; it is light that I so choose.
So please let me help you eliminate these sad and cruel untruths.

Did you know that I could take your pains and lovingly heal your wounds,
cast a few spells to make you rid yourself of guilts, regrets, and rues,
light a candle, make a tea, transmute your lowly blues?

'Tis true, dear friend. 'Tis true!

I can take your broken heart, patch, and make anew,

dismantle outdated notions, those hurtful and misconstrued.

My magic is not for the masses, but a small and counted few.

So, I carefully ask you, once again, do you believe this to be true?

Do you believe that I can make your world beautiful and new?

Do you believe in magic? Say you do! Please, say you do!

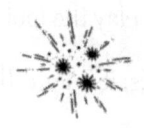

...And Sometimes Nice

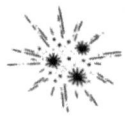

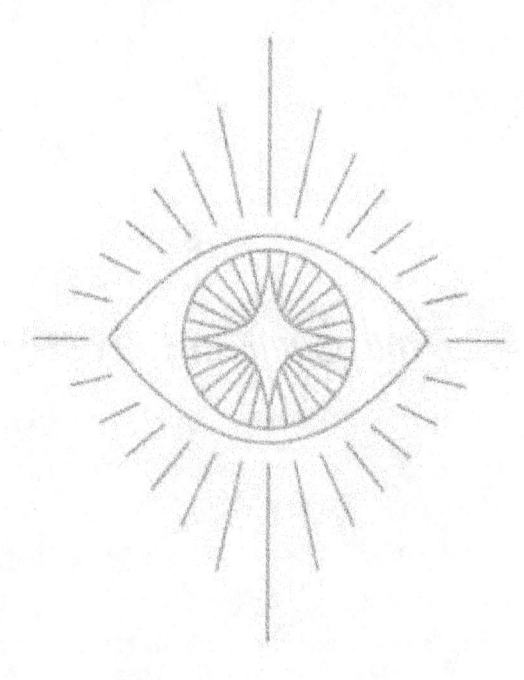

The Colors of the Adriatic Sea

Hershey-colored kiss

Honey-glazed goliath

Sultry sugar daddy

Mocha cappuccino

Caramel-covered casing

Darkened dolce dermis

Cafe de olla caliente

Mediterranean *vino*

Brown sugar beast

Cinnamon-sprinkled skin

German chocolate gent

California brown bear

Decadent brownie bundle

Tall glass of pinot noir

Peanut butter prince

Almond joy affair

Catrín de cacao
Xocolatl Xochipilli
Kahlua mixed medley
All lovers beware!

Dulce de leche, sands of *Campeche*,

hand over the Adriatic Sea

into the hands of Aphrodite

where she is ultimately free

to paint in Venustian waters.

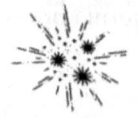

Eudaemonic

Life is like a bag of chips.

    Instinctively, I gravitate towards the fractured pieces

        while the rest of the world takes what's afloat.

            Yet, those broken bits bewitch me.

My fingers sink to the bottom of the bag,

    searching for the uncared-for crumblings,

        the maimed remnants of *maíz,*

            those that always seem to be left for last.

I pinch them as if possessing

    a precious piece of copal between my fingers.

        I soak them in my savory salsa

            with visions of reviving their spice of life.

And before I drop them onto my tongue,

    I, timelessly exhale the breath of life,

        making them whole once more.

            And that — makes me happy.

The Unfleshing of Mere Mortals

Her front door is, indeed, a magical and mystical portal

for many-a-lover

deemed undercover

as the love-making Goddess begins to turn mortal.

The tobacco-colored hammock holds heavy, his scent.

The oversized chair

tells of tales oh-so-rare

while the bedroom ceiling fan grants its ceremonious consent.

The mirrors, they capture, every passionate moment.

The *Nahuales* gather to meet

when the couple falls asleep

to consent, approve, grant permission, and condone it.

Lover-infused sheets make the Goddess weak-in-knee.

Passion drips down showers.

Clocks forget to mark their hours.

Celestial chimes and heavenly trumpets wake the lovers with glee.

Spiders spinning clockwise, rejoicing every encounter.

Furry felines peek and flash

before they bolt and make a dash

as the lovers now invade the marble kitchen counter.

After rapturously refueling body, mind, and spirit

lovers run away

in a mesmerized kind-of-way

while the Goddess then prepares for her ensuing mortal visit.

Catch Her if You Can

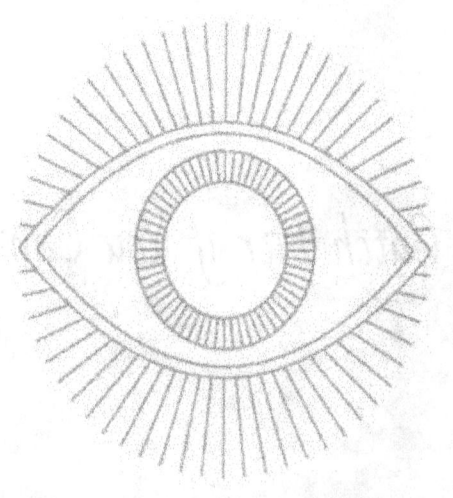

When the West Met His Wild

You may be the West, but honey, I'm the Wild,

the unruly rebel, unhitched hippie, untamed honey child.

I'm the tumble to your ever-rolling weed,

the heat-thriving rattler that frightens your steed,

rattling up monsoonal storms whenever there's a need.

You may have your Stetson's, but I have these-them, steel-toe boots.

And honey, you know very well, we're working in cahoots.

"These boots were made for walking...," please tell me, you know the rest.

Tell me you have some intuition and you've heeded its behest.

Could it be that you like the state chaos and permanent, civil unrest?

Perchance my Wild has finally infiltrated your pure and wholesome West.

Maybe you've come to realize, I'm your occidental best,

and you've seen the gleam of the crown that sparkles on my crest.

Now, now, now! I'm not saying I'm leaving behind the rest.

I'm just offering a little piece of home nestled between my breasts.

Take it or leave it, Mr. West. This journey is by no means mild.

Let me recapitulate — I'm your crazy, crazy Wild,

the unruly rebel, unhitched hippie, untamed honey child.

~ He took one long, good look at me, winked his eye, and smiled. ~

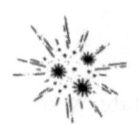

Love in Times of Quarantine

'Tis not a great love novel

simply the story of an average Adam and Eve

seeking paradise while in its midst.

No steamboat anchored downriver,

only years of patience stifled even further by a virus.

They both shared a peculiar relationship with the Universe

—a cruel-sense-of-humor type.

2020—the greatest epitome of them all!

The untouchable crowned jewel.

Hence, leaving them with only these:

    charming chats

        daring DMs

            and

                tantalizing texts.

In the words of Skip, it forced them to, "Slow Down"

for absence makes the heart grow fonder.

What a draconian lesson!

Prolonged sighs.

Extended urges.

Iztaccihuatl is on the brink of eruption.

Physical contact is but a dream.

And though impossible it may seem,

¡Sueña Mexicana! ¡Sueña!

For in the art of dreaming all wishes shall be redeemed.

Odd Night

Went to sleep fully clothed

atop a naked bed

every window tightly closed

and a blanket underhead.

Woke up with a crooked neck.

From the night before, a text unread,

which clearly explains the restlessness.

"*Buenas noches,*" the message said.

Apparently so because I woke up exhausted.

Dream on, my lover! Dream on!

Sweet to the Sweet...

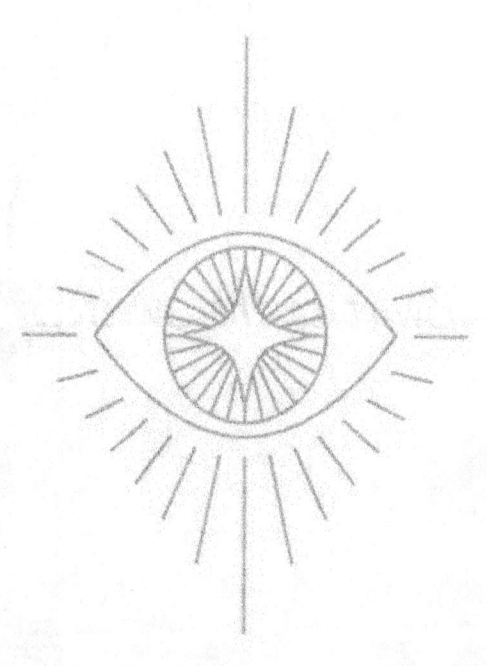

I'm in Love with...

German—

the sweetest thing,

smooth criminal,

decadent and delicious,

browner than my skin,

melts in my mouth,

topped with whipped cream

—Chocolate!

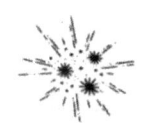

Hipoglucemia

Existe, en mí, un gran desequilibrio
por andar en ayunas, buscando asilo.

Me falta de mi fuente de energía
que me da vida y me llena de alegría.

Sufro de temblores y somnolencia
por existir tanto tiempo con su ausencia.

Me falta beber de sus mieles encantadoras
antes de que me consuman estas hieles trastornadoras.

Ocupo mi inyección de epinefrina,
de grandes cantidades de insulina,
de aquello que aumenta mi adrenalina.

Ámame pequeño duende, dueño de mis Zucaritas resucitadoras,
tú que tanto juras que me amas y me adoras.

~Miel de abeja que mis males aleja

~sacarosa santa que me revives y me levantas

~fuente de fructosa que veneras a esta Diosa

¡Cúrame de esta hipoglucemia!

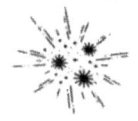

Chocorrol y Bon-Bon

A two-piece puzzle

that fits to perfection

fourré à la crème avec guimauve,

sweet to sweet,

brown on brown,

chocolat sur chocolat.

Así como la Diosa manda.

¡Caramba!

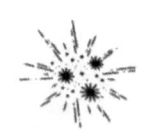

I Scream for Ice Cream

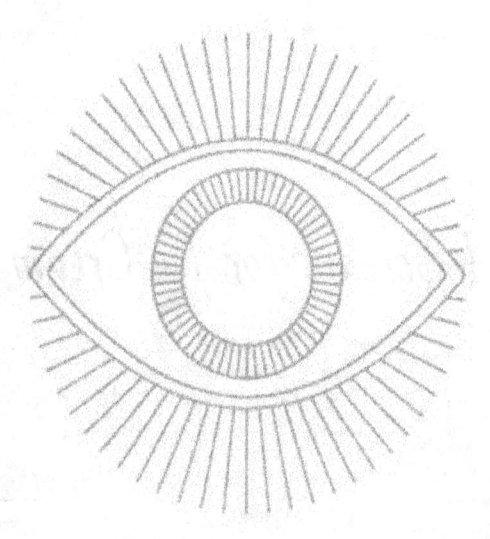

I'd Rather Have Ice Cream for Dinner

This ice cream comforts and soothes my soul,

renews my spirit, resets my goal,

keeps me ever-grounded, Earth to soul.

It numbs away all the pain,

freezes each cell and every membrane,

grants permission to be insane,

baptizes with mint chips as rain,

prompts in me more verse and refrain,

helps forget what-ever-his-name.

Holding onto a unicorn's mane,

ride like the wind, mystical dame.

Fría

Porque solo la nieve

apacigua

el fuego que llevo dentro.

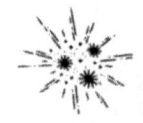

Just Two Tubs of Ice Cream

Soon the servings started to drip-drop,
as the cool summer evening quickly grew hot.

Drizzling in delirium and devious delight,
as citronella candles danced at the sight.
Oh, what a night!
Ooohhh, what a night!

He screamed.
She screamed.
La, la, la, la la!

The melted ice cream became one.
The Native Treaties had suddenly begun.

She screamed.
He screamed.
La, la, la, la la!

The melted ice cream became one.
The Native Treaties had suddenly been won.

With the rising of a new day's sun,

the two tubs of ice cream now had none.

Scrape the bowl. Lick the spoon.

Maybe a refill at the next full moon?

Too soon, my dear, too soon!

La, la, la, la, la.

The Native Treaties were now undone.

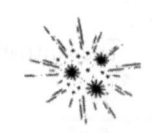

Café con Pan

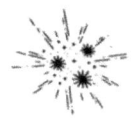

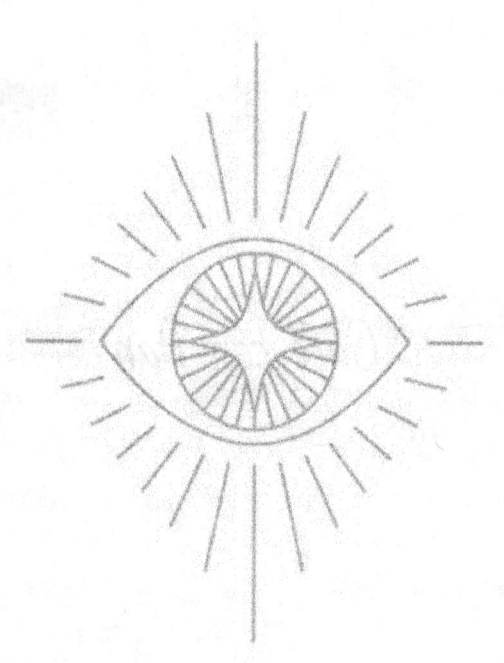

Café de la olla

Sweet aroma screams of *México*.

Bubbling brew boils over and over again.

Hints of *canela* to cure *la diabetes*

caused by the overdose of *piloncillo*,

unrefined brown sugar.

Unrefined indeed.

Your cure, the poison.

The poison, your cure.

But you love to dance with the devil.

You love to swim in muddy, brown waters.

Piel canela.

Panocha candente.

¡Uy!

Café de la olla caresses.

Lil Red and Mr. Lobo

Lil Red on her route,

oblivious to the world,

stopped by big, bad wolf,

who thirsting desires

to drink her up like morning coffee.

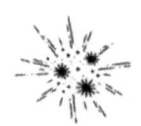

San Pan

Como no se come carne

en cuaresma,

mezclemos el queso panela

con la dulce panocha,

y comamos capirotada.

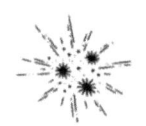

Pan con Café

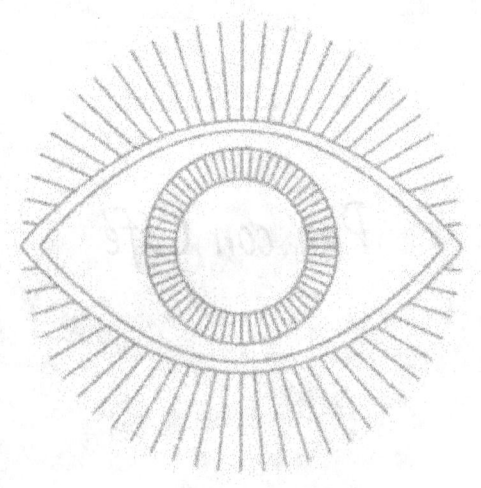

Moist

brown all over

rough around the edges

ooey-gooey

moist in the middle

~ La Brownie

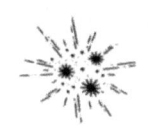

El Jaguar

The soft white granules under feet

allow me to sink deep within

as the lulling waves

lullaby me to slumber.

Hark, the shadows of the night!

There is a predator beyond the palms,

one that only I can see.

The jaguar lurks in the penumbra of *Tulúm*.

My mind's eye sees its yellow-red eyes,

the eyes of a *nahual*

and oh, how it thirsts for me!

Café de la olla (sequela)

Hay una olla de barro rojo

que hierve con alborozo

una y otra vez.

Pues nunca le falta leño

ya sea domesticado o fuereño

que la caliente cada mes.

Encendiendo aquella hoguera,

enchinando piel canela,

revoloteando canicas al revés.

Hay una olla de barro rojo

que hierve y hierve a su antojo

como si cada hervida en esta vida

fuera la última vez.

Esta Noche, Cena Pancha

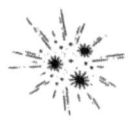

Engage

E-ntertain my

    N-octurnal desires

        G-rab hold of my

            A-morous fires

                G-racefully

                    E-liminate the lustful desires

-   that reside deep within

Palabras sabias

"En boca cerrada no entran moscas,"

palabras sabias de los abuelos.

Pero yo nací dionea, Venus atrapamoscas.

Soy planta carnívora que devora

carne embriagada de mentiras.

Mi saliva se desliza suavemente

sobre las pieles libidinosas.

Entre mis labios se disuelven los cuerpos

candentes de la verdad.

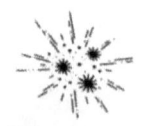

Ambrosia

I love to taste the taste

of your lips upon my lips.

Swipe that sweet nectar

from your tongue

onto mine.

Deliciously divine!

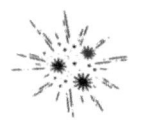

Y Pancho También

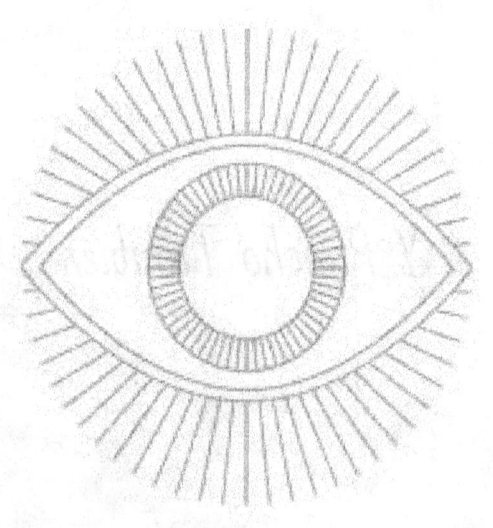

La lengua del amor

Hazme el amor con tu lengua,
con esa lengua elocuente que me susurra dulcemente al oído,
lengua que transforma las palabras más sencillas
en un manjar de sílabas suculentas y sensuales,
con esa lengua que empieza con palabras civilizadas y termina con gemidos salvajes.

Hazme el amor con esa lengua antigua,
esa lengua sabia y profética,
esa lengua, portal hacia el mundo esotérico,
donde las polaridades de la liberación y la atracción
suelen existir al mismo tiempo,
donde mutuamente damos y recibimos,
siendo simultáneamente masculino y femenino,
donde nuestras secreciones corporales forman un mar de amor,
profundo e inmenso.

Hazme el amor con esa lengua indígena,

lengua de nuestros antepasados,

que me transporta a un mundo muy lejano que aún vive dentro de mí,

que unifica todas nuestras vidas pasadas en el presente perpetuo,

haciendo que nuestros corazones formen un solo latido,

inquietando al cuerpo con el deseo de danzar al ritmo del sexo sagrado,

donde no solo existe la penetración física, sino también la penetración espiritual.

Hazme el amor con esa lengua mágica,

esa lengua que recorre mi cuerpo como un diccionario delirante de dichos desafiantes,

estimulándome desde la glándula P hasta aquel conocido punto G,

esa lengua erótica que se desliza suavemente sobre mi piel,

estremeciendo hasta las más íntima célula de mi cuerpo,

provocando el desborde de mis mieles encantadoras,

el néctar de esta Diosa, éxtasis encarnada,

que da a luz, en su orgasmo catártico, al paraíso,

un paraíso que ni Adán ni Eva llegaron a conocer,

donde todas las lenguas de todos los mundos

se funden para formar un solo idioma—

impecable e incondicional AMOR.

Pandemic Pussy

You trust no one.

Locked away in your home.

Isolated from every possible human.

The world is not safe,

except for the Goddess' crimson cove.

For some strange reason,

you forget about the pestilence

when it comes to her pink lady.

All other cherries are in contagion.

But not hers!

Goddess, no! Not hers!

And even if it were,

you're willing to risk any pandemic

for just one taste of her *panocha*.

Ya cállate y cómeme

No necesito de tu labia, necesito de tu lengua.

No me interesa escuchar tus monstruosas mentiras.

Mejor ven a deleitar tu endemoniado paladar

en mi mágico manjar

donde abunde la lujuria y toditita tu verdad.

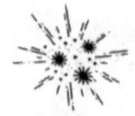

Viva México

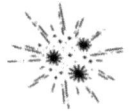

La Rumorosa

sierras rocosas

    carreteras curvosas

        amaneceres gloriosas

            cuevas misteriosas

                portal para las Diosas

                    hechizeras poderosas

                        sin maldad en el cuerpo

                          ni labia enredosa

                        rituales dolorosas

                    danzas religiosas

                mandas espantosas

            plegarias cautelosas

          seducciones hermosas

        entre curvas peligrosas

      para pieles pecadoras

   hiedras venenosas

y serpientes libidinosas

    ¡ay Diosa mía cuántas cosas

        se encuentran entre las sierras

            de la majestuosa Rumorosa!

Momma Likes Mexican

Tsssssss! Sizzle! Sizzle!

My mouth is drenched in drizzle.

Feelin' hot, hot, hot!

Sweatin' *la gota gorda.* on the spot.

Releasing steam from toe to head.

Hence, the pleasurable pains of REAL *enchiladas* in bed!

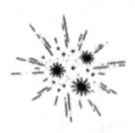

Ché chilangos chachareros

<u>El Chafirete</u>

¿Al chile que quieres enchufar el chucustrucus

con la chiquistriquis, mi china chacharera?

<u>La China</u>

En mi chante chupamos chelas y bailamos cha-cha-cha.

'Ta chido tu Chevy pa'l chaca-chaca, mi chafirete.

Bien chukisnais.

¡Al chile, mi chavo! ¡Al chile!

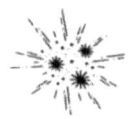

La Gira

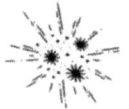

Blood Transfusion

{Momma needs new blood}.

It is required, indeed,

to eliminate his seed,

a uterine dilatation and curettage,

leaving her womb to bleed.

She needs to flush the toxins,

drink a *ruda* concoction,

injected by a new needle

to seal the past in a coffin.

To reverse the allergic reaction,

she must acquire a new satisfaction,

a novel and handsome prototype,

a transfusion of magnum attraction.

Momma needs new blood

to clear the void in her womb

after his extraction.

¡Arriba Jalisco!

- el feo tequila

- el chaparrito pp

- el que a la prima se la arrima

- el que sin nombre llegó y se fue

- el chente valiente

- y todos a los que al padre ya le confesé

Y así de sencillo,

sin salir de su recamara,

todo el estado lo recorrió

una y otra vez.

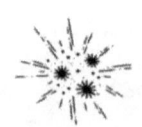

Trippin'

Took a twilight trip to Tijeras

to meet many New Mexican men,

then, to Texas to take on new exes.

carefully cutting the chords of when

a bear and his babe were barely just friends.

And now, in Amarillo, my answer. A-womb-men!

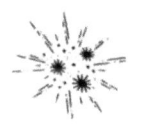

Enchanted

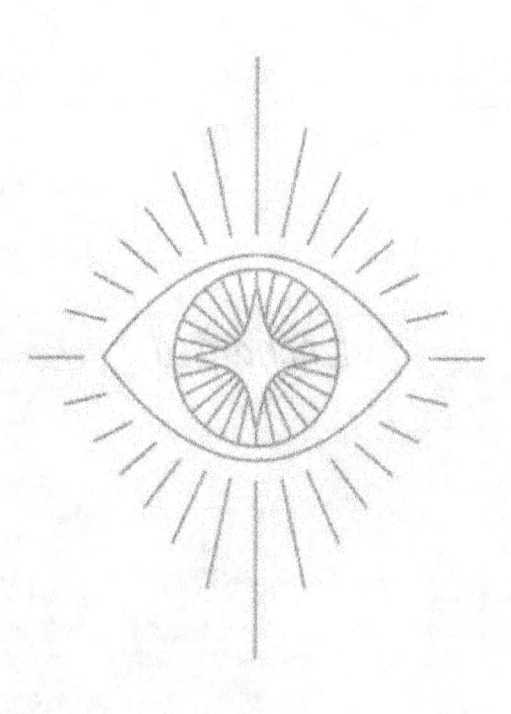

Incantation

EGYPTIAN GODDESS

OF HONEYDEW SKIN AND LUST

HOW I MISS YOUR TOUCH

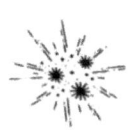

Eros and Psyche

Venus retrograde brings a wondrous lesson:

there is no greater love than to lay with a friend.

The soulmates are given a second chance

to express their love in the art of human form,

to consummate in body, mind, and spirit.

Love is divine, transcending space and time.

What is meant to be,

        ever was,

                ever is,

                        forevermore will be.

Impregnate Me

Fill me with your life, your brilliance, your passion,

your divine self which is overflowing with love and light.

Saturate each, and every one of my cells.

Help me to reach those higher vibrations

by allowing me to fly on the tips of your wings.

Brisas No, Solo Torbellinos

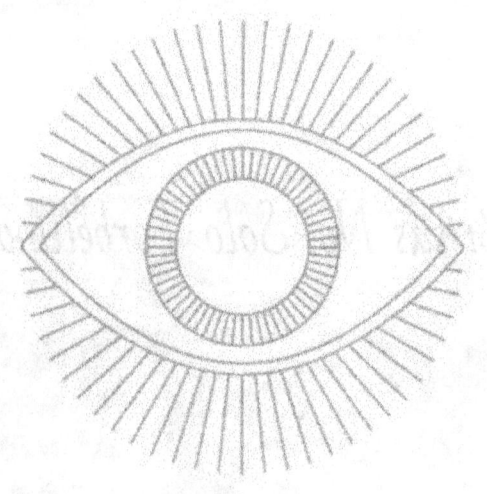

Lo que queda grabado

En una noche, como hoy

tocó una puerta oscura donde nadie lo vio llegar.

La única luz, aparte de sus ojos

venía de una recámara a medio brillar.

Las velas bailaban de emoción

 al ver dos sombras entrar.

Los ecos de aquellos, sus gemidos

vibraban por todo el hogar.

Sus delirios despertaban las fragancias del jardín.

Entre cortinas de seda fina,

se presenciaba una entrega sin fin.

Al despertar el sol, después de todo lo sucedido,

lo único que quedaba de ese encuentro indebido

~unas cuantas moraduras en el cuerpo,

~una pisada marcada en el sillón,

~ un hermoso recuerdo estampado

en un desdeñoso y esquivo corazón.

El cuento de una estrella fugaz

¡Ámame! mi niña.

Déjame ver el resplandor que escondes

en lo más profundo de tus pupilas.

Permíteme ser pasajero de tu nave espacial,

mi capitana cósmica.

Llévame a ese universo que es tan solo tuyo,

donde ni nada ni nadie existe,

más que esa especialidad enriquecedora

de tu amor incondicional.

Transpórtame a tu imperio erótico,

mi reina de corazones,

y hazme esclavo de todos tus placeres.

Accédeme alimentarme de tus mieles encantadoras.

Embrújame con tu mirada misteriosa

que me traslada a una galaxia desconocida.

Porque yo, a pesar de ser un gris,

a tu lado me convierto en camaleón de mil colores.

Siento desvanecer todas las sombras de mi existencia,

ya que iluminas lo más tenebroso de mi existir.

¡Ámame! pequeña muñeca,

aunque sea solo un día,

aunque sea solo una hora,

aunque sea por última vez,

pero, ¡ámame!

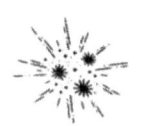

The Big Bang

La estrella y el lucero como buenos amantes,

solo en la oscuridad de la noche se encuentran.

De día van tan encandilados por el sol,

que en vez de juntarse, sólo chocan.

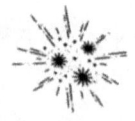

So Above, Below

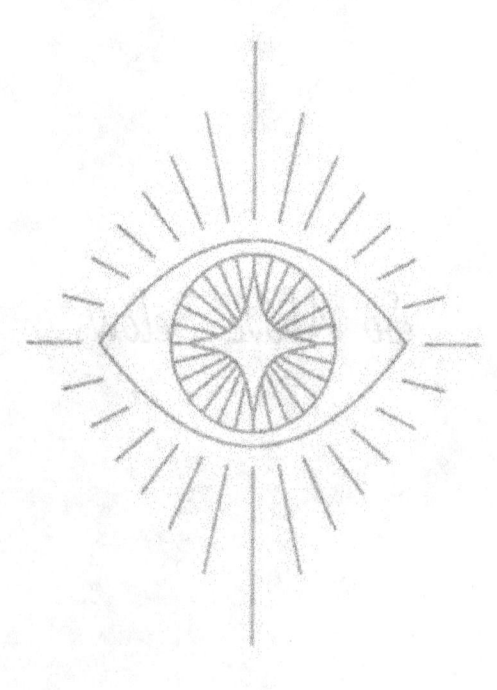

In Excelsis Deo

El cielo exaltaba tu nombre

como cuando entre gemidos

pintábamos las sábanas de fuego celestial.

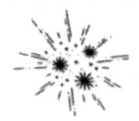

Want to Be

~where waves whisper wisterious words

    and the ocean obliterates all ostentation

~where sands cling like tattoos, sloughing off layers of societal stagnation

~where sins and saltwater sing symphonious songs of salvation

~where soft breezes and perspiration promulgate pervasive passions

~where juicy mangoes drip dreams of delirium and digressions

~where tequila tantalizes the throat,

    synchronisticaly summoning strangers in the night

~where mid-dark hours mesmerize the mermaids into sight

    ~where the sun kisses the sultry skin by day

        ~where the moon marvels at the wolf's devouring of its prey

            ~where the sirens return to their realms before light

~oy vey!

    ~still, I want to get away

    ~will you take me,

~s'il vous plaît?

Del Mar

Sing, sweet siren,

songs of seduction and *siniestras,*

where the sands are darker than the depths you swim.

Dear Oceanid,

Allure this sinful soul

into your curated and curvaceous caverns.

Allow me to linger in your libations,

losing myself in licentiousness.

Let us forget the sins of this man,

unless you are here to absolve me.

For if that is not the case, *nefasta* Nereida,

throw me upon your rocky shores

and cast the first stone.

Mea culpa! Mea culpa!

I willingly pay my penance

in exchange for living "le petite mort"

for just one night with you,

beautiful Magindara.

P is for Puta

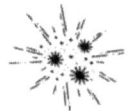

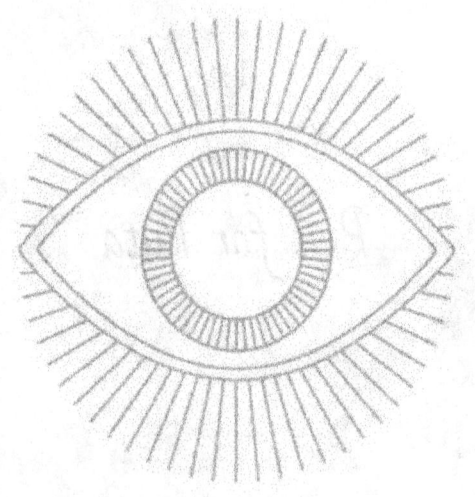

Pencaminosa

Me acusan de nopalera,

a prickly pear nopal,

llena de espinas peligrosas.

¡Ah, pero bien que tragan tunas!

I am accused of being unapproachable,

wearing a self-made crown of thorns,

donde en cada penca grabé sus nombres,

donde en cada penca grabé sus nombres.

Y en cada penca grabé sus nombres,

tatuados para siempre.

Poly

Poly wants a—nope!
She doesn't like crackers.
She ain't down with the pail and salty shit.
She prefers chocolate *conchas y puerquitos*.
Because she likes 'em brown and sweet.
She's got a sweet tooth the size of Texas, ya know?
Golosa como ella sola.
Y como uno no es ninguno
y de los tres no se hace ni uno,
that's why,
Poly wants the entire *panadería*.

P de perdición

Pin Pon es un muñeco
muy guapo y de color
sabor a chocolate
un hombre sabrosón

                                      Lo miro desde lejos
                                      me llama la atención
                                      que quiero ser su amiga
                                      sabor a colación

Pin pon dame la mano
bailemos el Danzón
el Tango y la Lambada
pretendo vacilón

                                      Pin ponme bien la mano
                                      con un fuerte apretón
                                      y bésame los labios
                                      con toda tu pasión

Pin ponme el cuerpo encima
perdamos la noción
que quiero ser tu amante
sin amonestación

> Pin ponme como quieras
> no lloro ni hago así
> por esta sola noche
> soy solo para ti

Pin ponme en tu memoria

que ya me voy de aquí

mañana vuelo lejos

pues soy un colibrí

> Pin Pon, mi gran muñeco,
> mi rey de seducción
> sigamos siendo amantes
> Pin Pon,
> Pin Pon,
> Pin Pon.

Al Rojo Vivo

Scarlet Skies

~~~

the color of

scratches

gnawed breasts

and a raw yoni

wild passions

beyond measure

with a futile desire

to penetrate beyond

all that is unseen

~~~

the color of

relentless rage

foolish drunkenness

and unconscious stupors

causing doors to slam

with midnight races

down a lonely highway

~~~

the color of

sandy portals

and dancing dolphins

transforming a sensual lover

into growling-grunting beast

sniffing at his prey

~~~

the color of

a midnight mistress

and a vampire king

who hated to love

but loved to hate each other

within the depths of darkness

in a sea of blood

~~~

the color of

a moon-dripped bed

where pain and pleasure commingled

with volatile tenderness

where her presence was heard

from miles away

yet her departure

silent as snow

~~~

the color of

extremes and regrets

an endless ocean of tears

that like the tides

ebbed and flowed

at times serene

at time tsunamic

but never safe nor soothing

Sangria Seductions

To the vampire king of midnight affairs,

    Dip that black magic brush into my crimson cove.

    Let us splash berry blossoms on the bed.

    Smear the sheets with sacred stains.

    Celebrate my scarlet ceremony.

    Let us toast, my vampire king,

    victim and prey of my sangria seductions.

XOXO,

Your Midnight Mistress

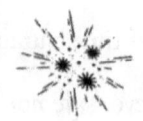

Raw

like a spring break sunburn

blistering hot

unrefined and fully alive

al rojo vivo

scraped up knee

inhaling O2

unpolished, uncut stone

rough and tumble

como carne asada a la parrilla

sizzle, sizzle, slide

oh, the painful pleasures

of being by your side

The Freaks Come Out at Night

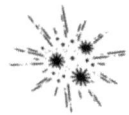

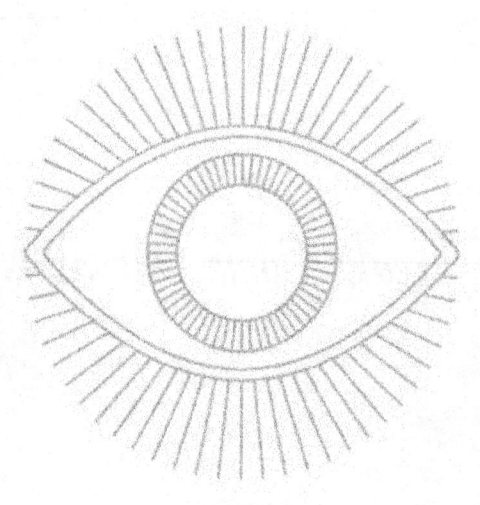

The Bewitching Hour

It's 3 A.M.

and my eyes finally put an end

to the game of "let's pretend we're sleeping."

My phone,

which should be in "do not disturb" mode,

allows his texts to come through.

It's 3 A.M.

and it is as if he knows that nothing is dormant in my house,

as if I am subconsciously awaiting an early morning rendezvous,

and this creature seems to speak my subconscious language.

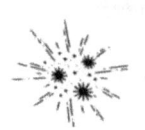

La Mari Mota

Mari Mota,

mujer loca,

más se enciende entre más la toca.

¡Qué poca—Madre Santa!

A la sacerdotisa bien que le encanta.

Hierba misteriosa, sagrada planta,

hojas mágicas que re-levantan.

Globito rojo que estás en los cielos

entre fuertes chillidos y deslumbrantes centellos.

Pero, Caperucita no deja de sonrojar

al ver que el lobo feroz la observa sin descansar.

Cuanto calor, que falta de aliento,

cuan indecoroso es el resto de este cuento.

Colorín colorado, aún no ha acabado,
sigue en busca de su próximo amado.

Así que, a La Mari Mota, se las dejo a su imaginación,
entre humos intoxicantes y perdiendo toda razón,
desvaneciéndose, todo el mundo, por falta de respiración,
sabiendo que en el sentido espiritual, esta situación,
es simplemente una más de su efímera colección.

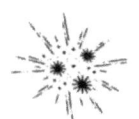

Nightmare

Allow me to be your greatest nightmare.

You know,

the kind that keeps you up at all hours of the night,

stimulating hypervigilance and detrimental delight,

provoking perfidious palpitations,

giving way to hallucinogenic hesitations,

those that begin by pounding on the chest,

and in their attempt to escape,

strangle your Adam's Apple at my request.

One, two,

I'm coming for you.

I'll make you toss and turn, drenched in a cold sweat,

Daggers to the heart, lest you ever forget.

Three, four,

you'll be begging me for more

as I make you scream in the dead of night

while you surreptitiously surrender in a paraplegic fight.

Five, six,

I will use your magic stick

—against you,

casting sinful spells which will create chaotic convulsions.

The more you try to resist, the greater my expulsions.

Seven, eight,

your pain will be great.

Hark, the evidence on your neck when you awake!

And for heaven's sake,

don't be fooled into thinking I am yours to take!

Nine, ten,

you'll want to relive this again and again,

dying for one more night

filled with painful pleasure and oxymoronic fright,

never wanting to close your eyes

when...

Good night! Good night!

Proceed with Precaución

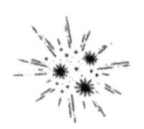

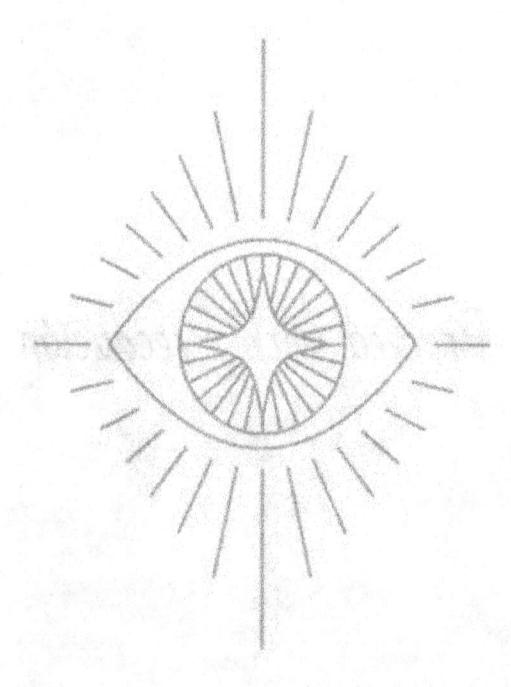

WARNING

Stand back! Don't come near,

'less you want to know the real meaning of fear.

You're clueless to the kind of work I do, my dear.

Wasn't born yesterday, not that innocent.

You're a wolf in sheep's clothing, that's clearly evident.

It's time you get to steppin'.

Ain't got no time for messin'

with your 3D desires of undressin'.

Thinkin' you could teach me a lesson?

Boy, you don't shit!

A minute with me, you won't know what hit.

You about to make this dragon woman spit

FIRE!

Cuidado

Más peligroso

es una mente cerrada

que una boca abierta.

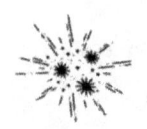

Beware!

I am not HIS-panic!

I am not HER-panic!

I am everyone's PANIC!

Finger-on-the-trigger.

And I am not talking about guns.

My poems are the weapons.

My words are the bullets.

And you, you are my trigger!

Beware! 'Cause I just might shoot!

S-P-E-L-L-I-N-G Be

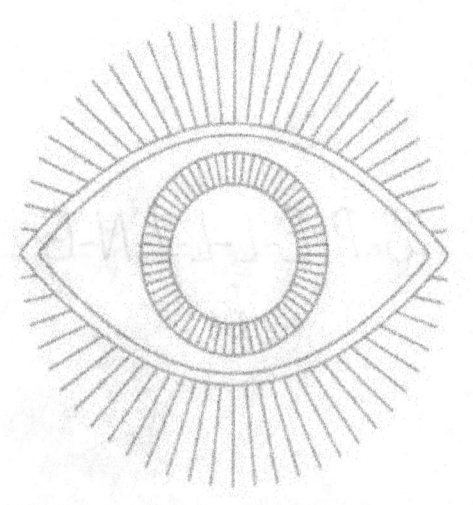

A Plague on Both Your Houses

Dante and Diana dance in the dimly-lit den

Sinful swaying mixed with scents of sacred smoke

A comfortable couch, the culprit of cooing and cuddling

Double doors leading to devious delights

Pigeons pitter-patter on the rooftop

As the sun sounds the alarm on Sinai

One more round of ravishing rewards

Banana pancakes proclaim a piece of paradise

Followed by a carefully crafted cup of Joe

Wiping away the wife's weeping tears

Emotions evolving to and fro

Too soon to try to leave or go

To meditate on the murder of Mercucio

Orthography

S- So you think you can just walk away?

P- Please, sunny boy!

 —You're not in control.

E- Everything:

 every thought,

  every reaction,

   every moment in time

    you perceive has been meticulously

     calculated and pre-ordained.

L- Love me.

L- Leave me.

 —I decide.

  Because I'm the one!

   Yes, sunny boy!

    I'm the one!

     SPELL it out!

Became

You be comin' after me for years on end.
I be runnin' away, runnin' away, runnin' away.

You be comin' for my heart over and over again.
I be pushin' away, pushin' away, pushin' away.

You be cummin' with me for the very first time.
I be cummin' on you day-after-day, day-after-day.

You becomin' a permanent fixture in my often-changin' world.
I becomin' your God-damned fool with whom you play, with whom you play.

You becomin' a vulgarity coming out of my filthy mouth.
I becomin' the thing that you most hate to say, most hate to say.

I became the first of many firsts,
managing to quench your insatiable thirst,
the one who was able to, your bubble, pop and burst,
whose name will be tattooed on your heart when they take you away in a hearse.
Whether you be comin', be cummin', or becomin'
I'm the one who, in the end, became your greatest curse.

Did Someone Say Bruja?

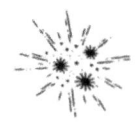

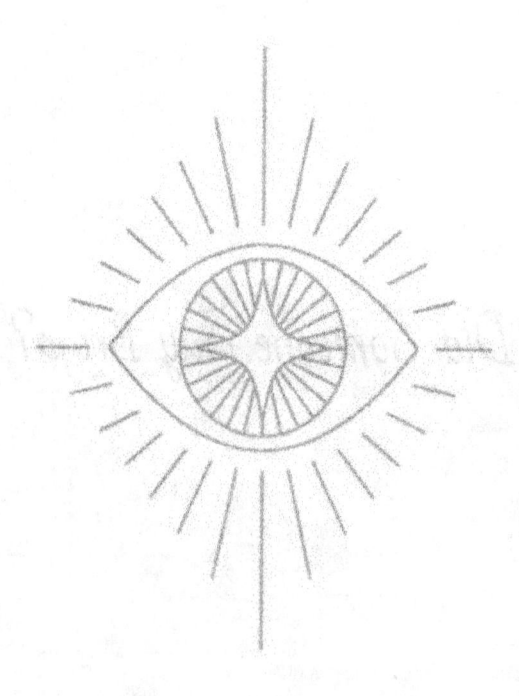

Leta-mía

Ave María Puri-fica a la pecadora

quemen, en vivo, a esa señora,

amortigüen la voz de la colorida lora.

Ave Mari-onetas que tartamudean

que con sus santos rosarios, a la mujer, la rodean

y repetidamente, sus pechos se golpean.

Ave Ma-la saña, esos cuentos indecorosos

creando entre la multitudes pensamientos morbosos

enfureciendo a las esposas por provocar a sus esposos.

Ave-s que vuelan repartiendo tanto chisme

de que en California, una bruja, verdaderamente existe.

la que con tan solo unas palabras, al hombre, lo desviste.

¡Ave María Purísima!

Ya se hartó la bruja bellísima.

"Que a sus memorias les llegue un borrón,

a sus corazones de hielo, un soplón,

y que esas lenguas envidiosas se conviertan en chicharrón".

Y con su varita mágica, esas mismísimas palabras,

en hechos las convirtió.

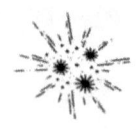

Today, I Killed a Tarantula

It was a furry, fiery-colored spider.

Cause of death: squished by a window.

What was it doing on my car?

Why was it creeping so near?

Motive: accidental.

I swear there was no intention to kill!

It was simply in the wrong place at the wrong time.

Or, was it?

And there it stayed lodged between the window and the sill

for several days,

like a trophy,

as if announcing to the world,

"Don't fuck with this *bruja*!"

El embrujado

Se me enchinó toditito el cuero
cuando el Chino se me encueró
y la vieja bruja de su madre
muy bien que me lo embrujó.

¡Quédese usted con su hijo
que su ADN, ya me lo dio,
el día en que se me enchinó el cuero
cuando su Chino precioso se me encueró!

Welcome to My Jungle

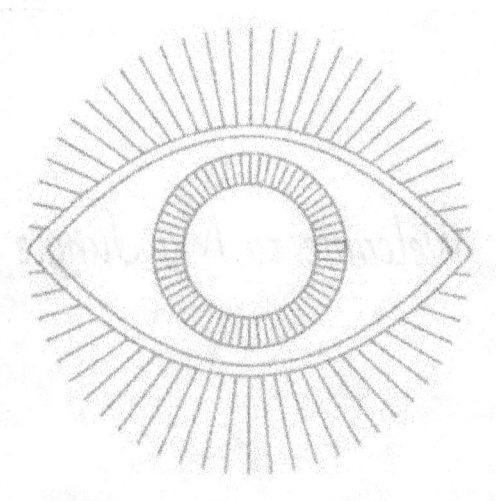

La selva te llama...

Selva sagrada

serpiente de la ceiba

señorita del sexo

sensualmente salvaje

seduciendo a los siniestros

los cínicos malvados

Los siembra y los encierra

en raíces bajo tierra

que se arrepientan de sus pecados

y paguen caro su condena

Cada burro, asno y buey

en los brazos de la encantadora

e infamada Xtabay

Felina

You don't know how to approach her...

"Too fucking scarey," you say.

Pues, ¡¿qué chingados le hiciste güey?!

Aw!!! Did your little pussycat turn feral?

Did she turn her fertile womb sterile?

I wonder why...

Why is it, until now,

you discover the hidden jaguar within this *mujer dormida,*

this *mujer gigantemente, brutalmente encendida,*

who of all felid species has the strongest and most powerful *mordida.*

Damn right, *que ya sacó las garras para filetearte sin medida!*

You should be fucking scared *de esa poderosa, feroz felina*

a la que de nada, nadita de este mundo se le olvida

quien siempre manda y siempre domina

la que es capaz de cobrarte hasta tu última gota de vida.

Atentamente,

    La Feroz Felina

Bottom of My Soles

You are not a roster.

No fierce-fighting cock.

You don't even make it to chicken.

So much lower than I originally thought.

Tell the world what you really are

—I will, I must, I ought.

    Chicken shit

—that at the bottom of my soles,

    just happened to get caught.

You Thought

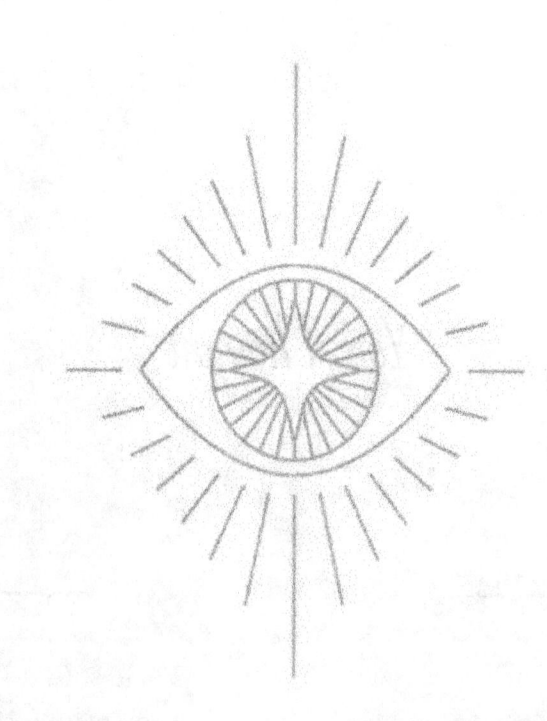

Shady Magik

Shady magik doth exist,

for it stalks my every move.

Hence, I question,

— Doth seeist this?

    How, your shackles, I remove?

    For I, too, know exactly how

    which shady magik to use.

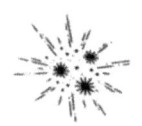

En camino

Huesito, huesito de chavorruco

tan verde y tan inmaduro,

se te va a acusar con el Gran Chuco

a ver con qué tipo de truco

le vas a salir para mentir

de no haber acosado a la pequeña Rubí

porque cuando tú apenas vienes,

yo ya te vi como hasta con tus ojos la querías desvestir.

Qué bueno que te caché

porque aquí no se baila el Tango con ninguna Bernabé.

Cuentas claras y enemigos a largas.

Ya te topaste con una Vargas.

¡Ya vas, cabrón! ¡Ya vas!

Al infierno con todo y zapatitos nuevos.

A ver, a ver, ¿no que eras de muchos huevos?

Ahora con la cola entre las patas,

huyendo de mi furia, arrastrándote a gatas.

¡Ya vas, cabrón! ¡Ya vas!

Peina'o pa' tras

pa' no volver jamás

agarradito de las garras del mismísimo Satanás.

¡Ya vas, cabrón! ¡Ya vas!

Voodoo

Who do?

I do?

Nah, boo!

You do!

Feel the rue?

The hate you spew?

I'm just reversing your fucking curse

multiplied by two!

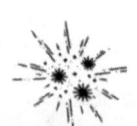

Unstoppable

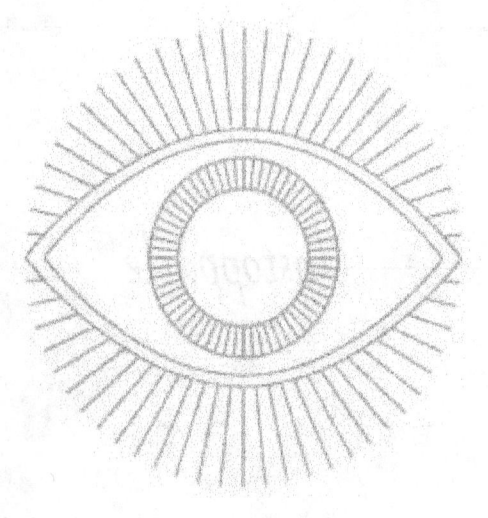

Candle Work

My candles keep on blackening,

sizzling, and crackling.

My rooftop guests keep cackling

in the middle of the night.

My candles keep on shattering,

cracking down, and clattering.

My closet guests keep hammering

attempting to build fright.

My candles keep on blackening,

sizzling, and crackling.

But I keep on keeping on fighting the fiercest fight!

Black Spiders

The brave black widow vigilantly guards the front door.

Delicate daddy long legs, meditates in the bathtub, forevermore.

Another one enjoys the luxury of cherry-covered towels.

Had to lay him to rest as he crossed the boundaries we vowed.

The infant bounces ever-so-slightly above the ancient books,

while others play peek-a-boo behind the closet's nooks.

Oh, the webs we weave,

the shapes we tend to shift!

Energies linger through the air

making moves that are noticeably swift.

Now is the time for prayers to hold fast,

catching the curses that have been cast,

willfully wrapping these woeful words

to finally break the spells, they thought would last.

Alas!

Armada

Regardless of the amount of poison,

my black spiders still march on.

Holy, Holy, Holy

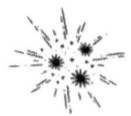

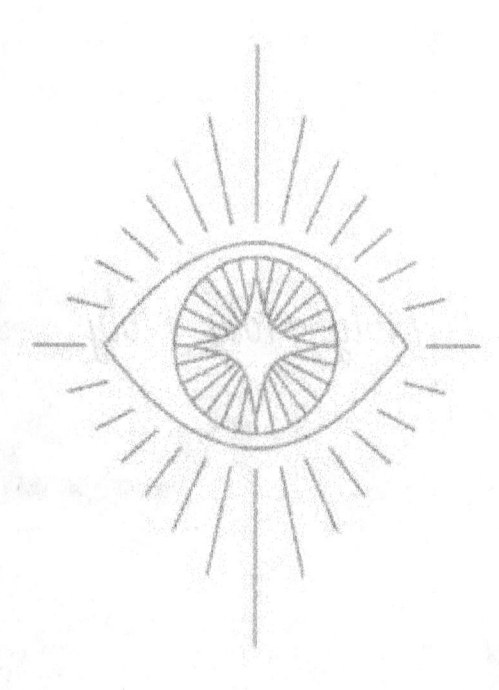

El padre y la puta

<u>Padre</u>

Te vas a ir al infierno por acostarte con un sacerdote.

<u>Puta</u>

Y tú te vas a ir al infierno por acostarte con una mujer casada.

Así que, ve haciéndonos reservaciones en el hotel de Gehenna.

El cuento más pequeño

Este es el cuento de un sacerdote que quedó ex comunicado

y la puta que se fue al infierno por seducirlo.

Uno quedó fuera de la iglesia

y la otra quedó fuera del paraíso,

siendo que ambos cometieron lo mismo.

Fin

—a la misoginia.

All Hail St. Michaela

St. Michaela, with sword in hand,

is ready to slay every Piscean man.

¿Ella puede? Oh yes, she can!

The Piscean Age is permanently over.

The Aquarian Era is finally here.

Those taking advantage of a misogynistic life

are now squirming and wreaking in fear.

An eye for eye; a tooth for a tooth!

Isn't that, simply put, your golden truth?

Oh! Now you find it distasteful and uncouth?!

The shoe, at present, is on the other foot.

So why, oh why do you fear that now?

The pendulum has swung to the other side,

and St. Michaela has taken a vow.

She is ready to maim, slaughter, and slay

any and all chauvinistic display,

then watch the outdated burn and decay.

All hail St. Michaela!

For she has come to save the day.

Putting an end to the privileged masculine.

Slay, St. Michaela!

Slay!

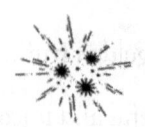

Truth Hurts

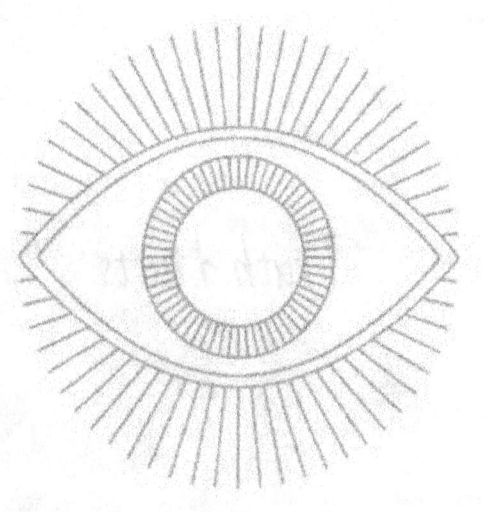

Ya no sé ni cómo ponerle

¿Y de qué me sirven tus, "I'm sorry," si no te tengo aquí,
si no has venido de rodillas a postrarte ante mí?

¿Y de qué me sirven tus, "I love you," si nunca has traído flores,
si nunca le has declarado al mundo que soy el amor de tus amores?

Cambia tu comportamiento. Háblame con la verdad.
Di que nuestra relación es mucho más que una amistad.

¡Oh, perdón! Pero es que tu no quieres compromiso.
Entonces no me hagas mosca. Hazte a un lado. Con permiso.

Yo no tengo ni el tiempo ni las ganas de enseñarle a un pequeño niño.
Lo que se necesita en esta vida lo llevamos las mujeres en el corpiño.

Hasta nunca corazón. Ojalá que te vaya bonito.
Aunque haya disfrutado entre tus brazos, la neta, no te necesito.

La dieta 3T

Estoy a dieta

-porque al consumirlos la panza me ha engordado,

-porque varias veces estos me han, severamente, quemado,

-porque por mucho tiempo los han hecho muy grasosos

 y entre mis manos, se me han vuelto muy resbalosos,

-porque sus contenidos provocan la alta presión,

 al igual que taquicardia y una severa depresión.

Yo no hablo ni de tacos, tortas, o tamales.

¡No mis damitas y seres cabales!

Estoy a dieta de los 3T, señoras y señores,

eliminando de mi vida tantas penas y mal sabores.

Porque de todo lo que he vivido y de todo lo que les he hablado,

mi dieta 3T consiste de tontos, tarugos, y tarados.

Sentí-miento

Consentimientos

Sin sentimientos

Lujuria total

"Femme fatale"

Porque ella no permite que la vengan a engañar

Ni siquiera con un solo hombre ella puede estar

Ni quiere

{Solo en el aquí y ahora está porque mañana, solo Dios dirá}

Con sentimientos de pasión

Va invocando cambios de estación

Convirtiendo del invierno más frío

En un arduo y empañado estío

Con sentimientos y consentimientos

Esos los tiene bien conocidos

Tipo que deja corazones destruidos

Esos que prometen la luna y las estrellas
Queriendo conquistar a las mujeres más bellas
Haciéndolas creer que son las únicas doncellas
Ella no puede con esa falsificación de huellas

Ni quiere

{Solemnemente va permanecerá pensando en su próxima conquista}

Con consentimientos
Sin sentimientos
Evitando sufrimientos
Saciando a los sedientos
Satisfaciendo a los hambrientos
Negando la construcción de falsos cimientos

Ella no sabe edificar hogares sentimentales
Ni siquiera puede imaginarse a los Cupidos celestiales

Y ni quiere

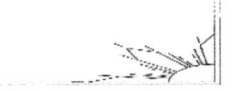

Justicia

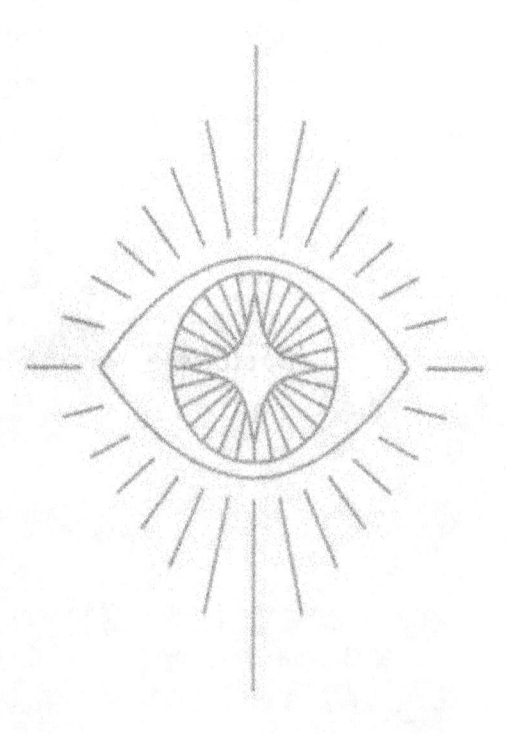

St. Michaela Presiding in the Case of Libra vs. *el Mudo*

"I don't know what to say!"

How about you don't.

Do as my grandpa used to tell us every day,

"En boca cerrada, no entran moscas".

Porque al fin de cuentas,

anything you do or say

will be used against you

in my court of justice.

Any questions, comments, concerns, or confusion?

He dicho.

¡Caso cerrado!

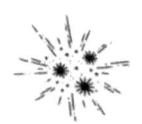

Todo con medida

Al morro le gusta la enchilada
porque así se calienta más.
Le encanta su salsa picosa
incomparable con nadie más.
Pero se le va a subir la bilirrubina
cuando ya no la pruebe jamás.
Tal vez hasta que eso suceda,
entonces, si, comprenderá
que no se le debe exprimir
o su salsera se agotará
y aquella bilirrubina
bien y bonito, se lo chingará.
No es que la picosa lo desee,
simplemente - sucederá.
De tanto comer enchiloso,
su mismo cuerpo se vengará.

Todo con medida, nada con exceso,
ya que las Diosas están muy bien protegidas
de los aprovechados del sexo opuesto.

The X m-en-tourge

Diosa X

eXed her partner

then heXed her eX,

the lying eXtraordinaire,

by eXorcizing the demons, he left behind

with the help of her X m-en-tourage.

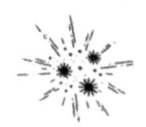

La Tequilera

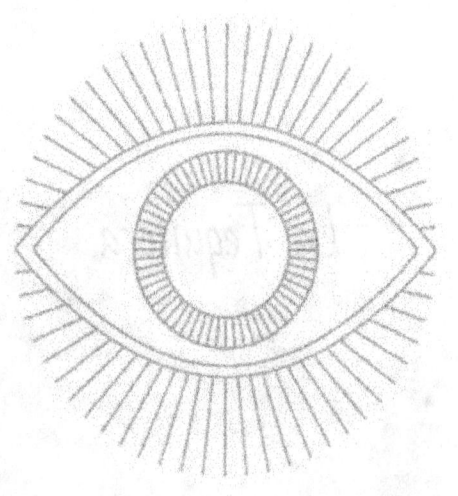

La Cruda Realidad

She introduced me as Diosa Equis.

Yet all he heard was Dos Equis.

He wasn't far too off!

I've been told I can be intoxicating,

producing hangovers that turn into hang-ups

which seem to hold on for years.

Cheers!

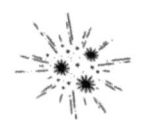

¡Salucita!

Soy cabrona, lo sé.

Sin pelos en la lengua,

ni vato que me mantenga,

vulgar y corriente,

libertina e indecente.

Sí, soy cabrona,

pero no porque dice la gente,

si no, porque a mí me importa

una pura y dos con sal

y después de esos tres tragos

me los enjuago con un buen mezcal.

¡Salud!

AMF

Gin

Mai Tai

Paloma

Hard Lemonade

Tequila Sunrise

Blended Margarita

but my favorite one of all...

Adios Muther Fucker

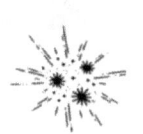

Hasta la Pasta

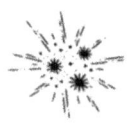

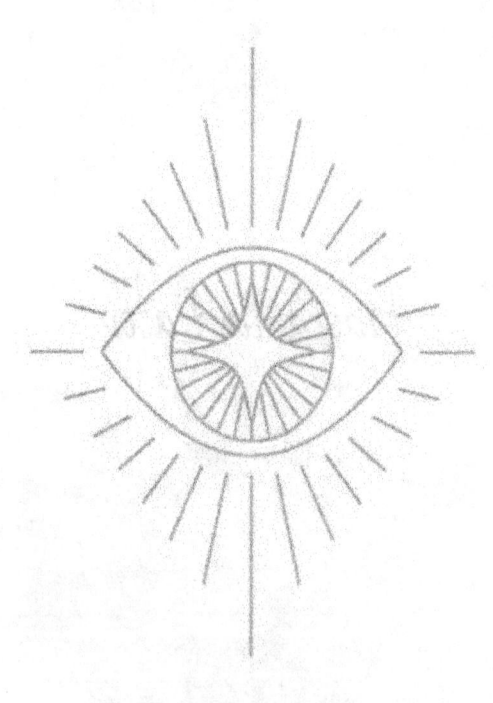

Diez amantes

Yo tenía diez amantes.
A los cabrones se les remueve.
Ya nomás me quedan nueve.

De los nueve que quedaban,
más mentiroso que Pinocho.
Ya nomás me quedan ocho.

De los ocho que quedaban,
el cobarde tenía machete.
Ya nomás me quedan siete.

De los siete que quedaban,
el mamón me borró del feis.
Ya nomás me quedan seis.

De los seis que me quedaban,
el celoso pegó de brincos.
Ya nomás me quedan cinco.

De los cinco que quedaban,

el maricón se largó con Nacho.

Ya nomás me quedan cuatro.

De los cuatro que quedaban,

se creía, del mundo, el juez.

Ya nomás me quedan tres.

De los tres que quedaban,

el boludo se fue con voz.

Ya nomás me quedan dos.

De los dos que quedaban,

en la Cárcel del Tribuno.

Ya nomás me queda uno.

De ese uno que quedaba,

'che vendido se hizo güero.

Ya nomás me quedan cero.

Entre perlas y diamantes,

se acabaron los amantes.

Pero ni tarde ni perezosa,

pronto se mueve esta Diosa.

La, la, ra, la, ra, larenta

mañana, empieza una nueva cuenta.

La, la, ra, la, ra, larenta

mañana, empieza una nueva cuenta.

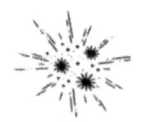

Las hieles de enero

Amarillo verdoso.

Sabor vilmente amargoso.

Un sentimiento profundamente doloroso.

Neta, que se me va a reventar la hiel contigo, ¡cabrón!

Y cuando se me pase la gran amargura,

y retome muy bien mi postura,

no me quedará más que repetir esta linda dulzura,

con las palabras de Ice Cube, que curan,

Bye Felicia!

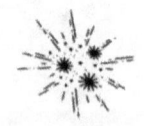

¡Tan! ¡Tan!

Todos los cabrones terminan en poema

No solo mi poesía, sino mi más grande lema.

Y tú, cabrón, ¿Cómo quieres terminar?

¿Quieres que divulgue lo que me hiciste sufrir y penar?

¿Acaso querrás que diga que fuiste el amor de mi vida?

Mejor les cuento como tu palabra de inmediato se te olvida.

¡Aaaah chinga, chinga!

¿Qué me creías, Santa Dominga?

No cabrón, ni santa, ni persignada.

De eso, te aseguro, que yo no tengo nada.

Tus mentiras, ve y cuéntaselas a tu madre o tu abuela.

Que aquí, en esta casa, ya no hay nadie quien te espera.

Pues yo no sé qué tipo de poema o poesía te esperabas

Yo no escribo fantasías ni tampoco cuentos de hadas.

¿Qué te parece si mejor te dedico estas mágicas palabras?
¡Júntate todas tus chivas y vete mucho a la chingada!

¡Colorín, colorín, colorado, colorado!
¡Este poema y esta "relación" por fin han terminado!

¡TAN! ¡TAN!

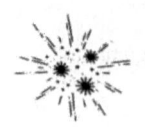

A la Chingada

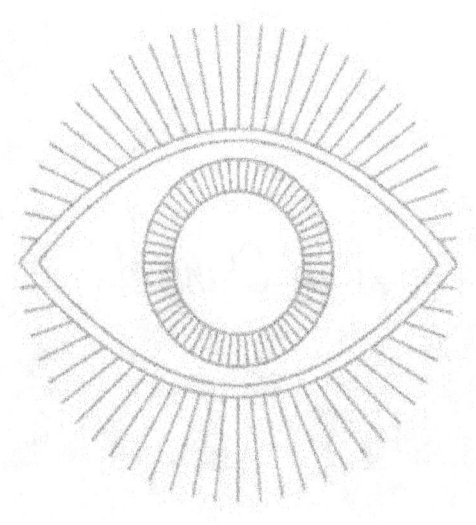

Butcher

I was not an educated professional.

I was not a dedicated teacher.

I was not a talented poet.

I wasn't even an attractive woman.

I was simply a piece of meat,

a pussy he wanted to fuck.

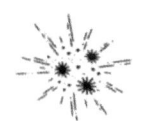

Evanesco!

I need substance not sex.

If I need a really good lay, I just simply call my ex.

In a matter of *un, dos, tres.*

¿Ya ves?

I don't need that virtual nonsense.

Don't come at me with no common sense.

Feed my mind; nourish my spirit.

Stay away from all that is violent and satiric.

Don't need a smart ass who loves rhymes and lyrics.

For I see through the eyes of an empiric.

You came knocking at my door, and I opened the window.

Noticing the inevitable development of a tsunamic crescendo.

No entiendo why you fools always end up in a match of kendo.

I am an ancient fighter. I know every possible ruse.

Before you know it, mid-first round, TKO, you lose.

Don't confuse me with your "stupid girls" as you like to call them,
for I have a crystal ball and tricks-a-dozen in my cauldron.

Yeah, I'm a *bruja*! Now what?!
Doesn't take me long to say I've had enough.

Thank you for reminding me that I am single by design.
For I have no greater love than that which is solely mine.
I define what is divine and choose whether or not to incline.

Evanesco!
For it is now the perfect time
to restore my peace of mind.
Evanesco!

Soiled

You, my lover, are just a seed.

But I, I am the fertile land that can either take that very seed

make it bloom or allow it to disintegrate within the moist soils of my womb.

I decide.

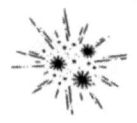

La Santa Muerte

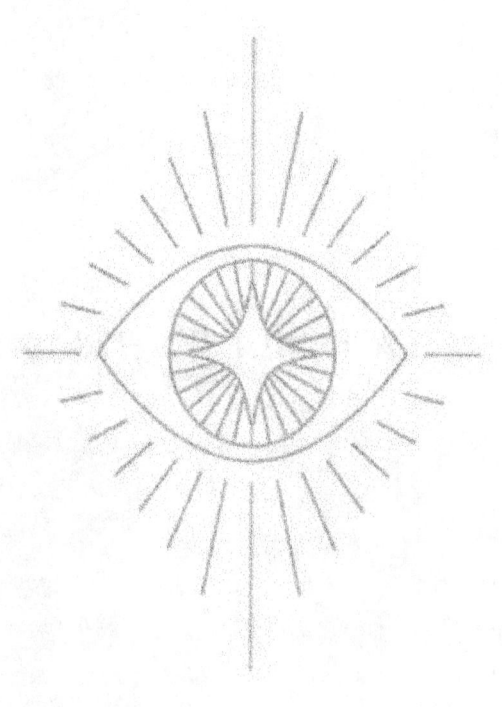

La Valentina

Ya llegó Valentina Domínguez,

la que con pistola en mano te dice,

"¡Ni me jodas, ni me chingues!"

¡Piú! ¡Piú!

Conejo Blas

Con tu escopeta

repleta de balas,

tú lo matas,

y a mí me salvas.

Santificado conejito,

te lo pido de favorcito.

Si le pegas de balazos,

te lo juro que resucito.

Sálvame de este infierno,

te lo ruego y te lo suplico.

Pégale de balazos

a ese lobo feroz y maldito.

¡Pas! ¡Pas! ¡Pas!

Mi querido Conejo Blas,

no sé cómo agradecerte.

Por fin descansamos todos, en paz.

Era del signo Libra

No cabe duda que la Muerte es del signo Libra.

~Justa y justificadora

~Cual viento sopla

~Aliento de vida

~Alimento del fuego

~Justiciera y ajustadora

Con la mano izquierda perdona,

y con el mazo en la derecha, detona.

¡Mazo! ¡Mazo! ¡Mazo!

Ni te atrevas en convencerla,

porque antes de que empiece el juicio

ya perderás tu caso.

These Ghosts Ain't Friendly

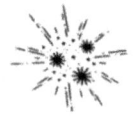

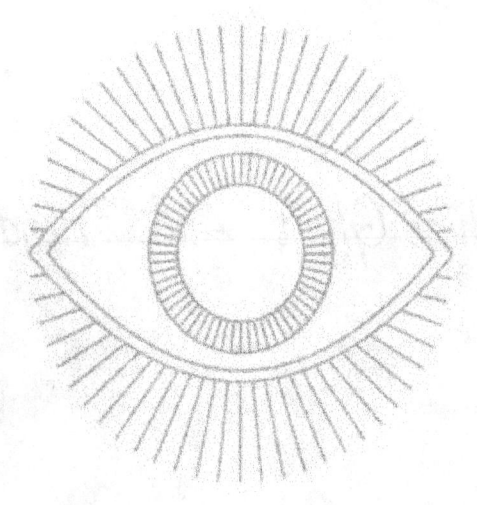

The Scariest of All

To love and be loved

is to walk through an abandoned mansion

in the middle of a thunderstorm

—always haunting,

full of ghosts,

scary as shit!

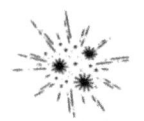

The Haunting

My eyes have been held hostage for over many hours.
As if the salt water, my iris, hungrily devours.

As though I cried enough tears to flood the River Nile.
But I haven't. I've been too busy living in denial.

I quickly swallowed super glue, wanting my heart to mend.
A pile of sticky fragments at my esophagus' end.

My big and bright heart chakra is motionless and pale.
My yellow solar plexus burns and aches without avail.

My entire body implores me to take a break and rest.
But I adamantly refuse to grant this much needed request.

I have no time for depression— to wait, to wail, and wallow.
I must not only bite the bullet, but take a deep breath and swallow.

I need to continue with life's activities and doings
Pretending my detrimental downfall isn't ensuing.

The anger and sorrow dizzy my head.

Yet, I know that I am not better off dead.

Because if that should happen instead

—I would really haunt you forever.

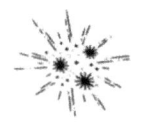

Ghosted

Oh no, dear honey, I don't ghost.

For ghosts are very much alive!

I just watch your memory roast

in my latest poems. No jive!

As you should know me true by now,

my homely ghosts are alive and well.

Don't even bother asking how!

You've heard them in my house so dwell.

So don't beg me not to ghost you

because my ghosts make lots of noise.

Hence, saying I don't ghost, 'tis true.

I simply carry on with poise.

My ghosts can come back from the dead.

To haunt you each, and every day.

I let them linger in my head,

anchored in poems, not astray.

I make, not, a single rumbling.

Simply write truths on every line.

To reflect on mistakes is humbling.

Go live your life and leave me mine.

I will silently disappear,

muted to you, forevermore.

Don't you ever come a-knocking.

I shall not open the door.

So don't beg me not to ghost you.

I'm not a revolving door.

Not like the women you're used to,

with me, it's over—nevermore!

Don't Close Your Eyes

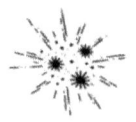

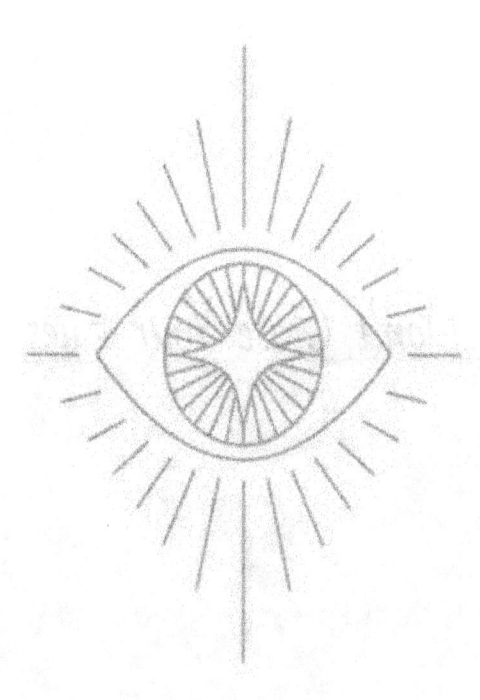

I've Finally Awakened from that Delusion

The bedsheets—in the trash.

The pictures—permanently deleted.

The coffee mug—to pieces, I smashed.

Incinerated red flags not heeded.

The book I read to try to understand

—a pile of ash in the chiminea.

The condoms—used up with another man.

I've become someone else's Dulcinea.

De ti, ya no queda nada.

                        You.

                                        Who?

Camarón que se duerme...

Te tardaste mi chavo. Yo ya me la curé.

Porque aquí no hay quien ruegue, pero sí quien dé.

¿Qué creías que te iba a esperar?

habiendo tanto taco de escoger para cenar.

Sea una orden o sean más de dos,

todos a la orden, y no me la hacen de tos.

En cambio, vos,

te tocó la de perder

porque nunca se le deja esperando a una mujer.

Ahora sí, ¿lograste entender?

Te tardaste mi chavo, porque yo ya me la curé.

Testament

Can I get a witness?

Please, tell me these ideas weren't inventions in my head!

Tell of how he stole my angels, leaving his demons on my bed.

Can I get a witness?

For his actions and reactions turned out to be all fake.

Testify against this so-called man who came to take and take.

Can I get a witness?

Please tell me that these words I speak are forthright and true.

Confirm to me how he cast a spell, sealing my eyes with glue.

Can I get a witness?

Verify the fibs, the untold truths, evasions and lies.

Prove to me I've not gone crazy, for I know that I am wise.

Can I, please, get a witness?

What's said and done is in the past. Let us look back no more.

Please, come be my witness and watch how Karma always keeps score.

Thy Queendom Come

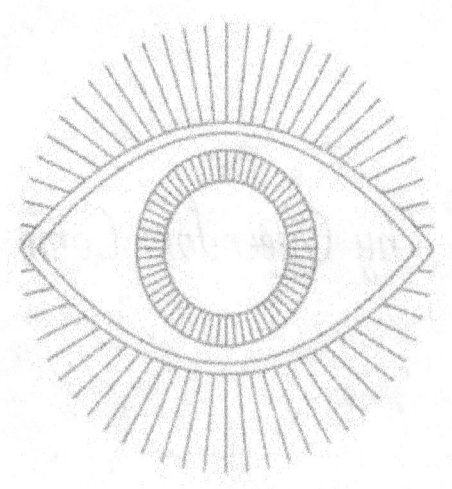

Not the Same

If I wanted, you'd still be in my bed.

But a girl's wants are not the same as a Goddess's needs.

SOUL-AWE

My solitary is NOT confinement.

SOLITUDE

I-DE-TU-SOL

your sun, my sun,
light of the world,
the Great I Am.

In my mind's eye,
conmigo misma,
I am supremely fine
sola con mi soledad,
my soul,
my light.

Soul-awe!
Sol-ahh!
Sola!

El reinado de la Diosa no tiene fin

Primero al pozo que tener esposo.

Que de maridos mareados, prefiero obstinar.

Porque esta coquetona prefiera andar de vaquetona

que ser sumisa, su mensa o muñeca con quien jugar.

Ave María, ¡esta putísima!

¿Esposada y condenada hasta el final?

¡Dios me libre!

La Diosa a de ungirme,

cuidarme y protegerme en su reino celestial.

¿Yo, tener esposo?

¡Qué castigo tan horroroso!

Si el océano es tan enorme, hay que saber pescar.

Ave María, ¡esta putísima!

¿Esposada y condenada hasta el final?

Que me encierren en calabozo que luego viene un vil baboso

a tumbar tanta barrera, queriéndome rescatar.

Ni sumisa, ni su mensa, ni una deuda en la cuenta

que esta Diosecita sus saldos sabe bien pagar.

Ave María, ¡esta putísima!
¿Esposada y condenada hasta el final?

Primero al pozo que tener esposo.
Y les pido de favorcito, que ya me dejen de chingar.

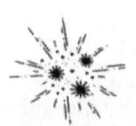

El Pilón
(porque el reinado no tiene fin, obvio)

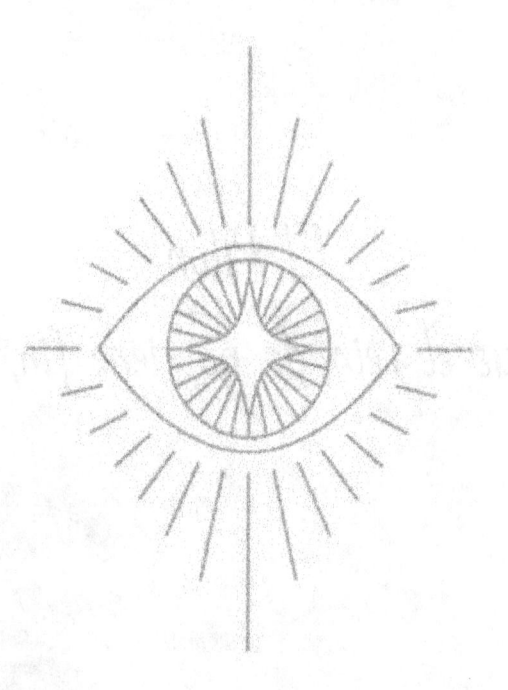

Entre las grietas

{Mis velas nunca mienten}.

Después

    de haberse esfumado,

        cristalinas y transparentes,

            el hollín empieza

                a hacerse presente.

Hay

    una fuga

        de obscuridad

           que se cuela

                por la atmósfera

                    de mi universo.

Hay quienes

    me creen tonta

        porque permanezco

           callada en la faz

                de la serpiente

                    ponzoñosa.

Me le quedo viendo,

        observando

                cada movimiento

                        sin temor y sin miedo.

Soy un espejo inmóvil,

        reflejando sus movimientos

                sin retroceder ni una pestaña.

Soy roca inquebrantable

        que se convierte en terremoto,

                espantando y ahuyentando

                        cual culebra que se resbala

                              por las grietas de mi ser.

Parto mi planeta

        por la mitad,

                permitiendo

                        que se lo trague

                              la tierra.

I Told You So

Missing the Magic?

So, you didn't have the time or the desire to stick around.

And now that time has passed, you search for what can't be found.

I told you so! I told you so!

I told you I made magic, and that I'd cast a spell.

I also kindly warned you, that only time would tell.

Tell you just how good you had it.

Tell about being loved and lost.

Do you wonder who's, now, loving it?

I wonder how much of your peace that costs.

Do you believe in magic?

Do you believe it to be true?

Do you wonder who's, now, loving it?

Not you, me dear! Not you!

Eclipse

On this day, I am finally able to
reduce your importance,
repute every inch of your skin,
and cast you into the shadows
forever.

The Effects of Excessive Chile

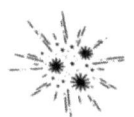

Reflujo

Mi amor ardía por ti,

pero ahora,

solo tengo agruras.

¡Ojo! ¡Mucho ojo!

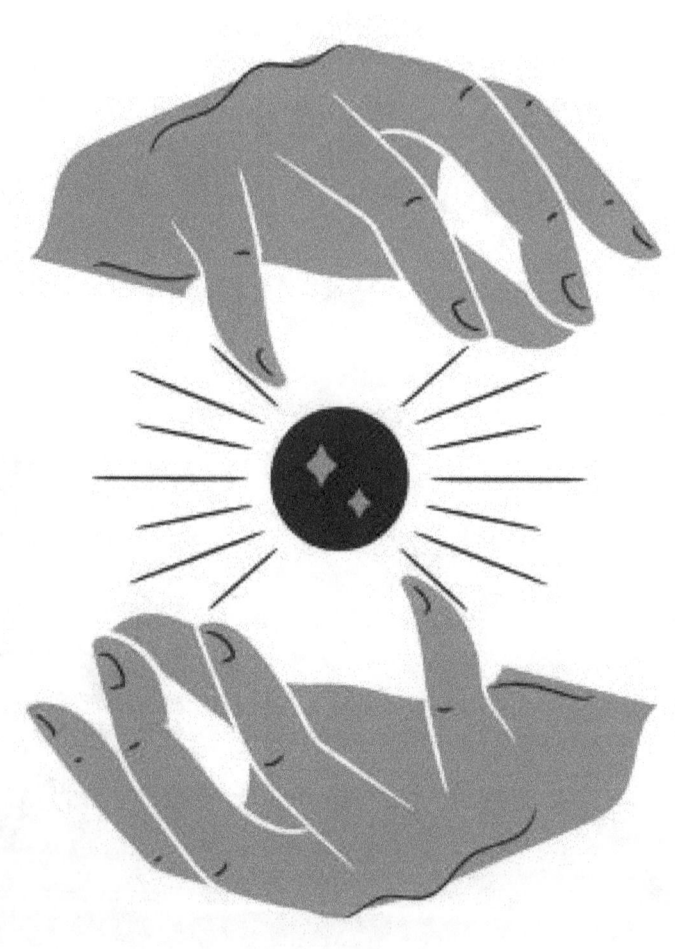

www.ingramcontent.com/pod-product-compliance
Lightning Source LLC
Chambersburg PA
CBHW071113160426
43196CB00013B/2559